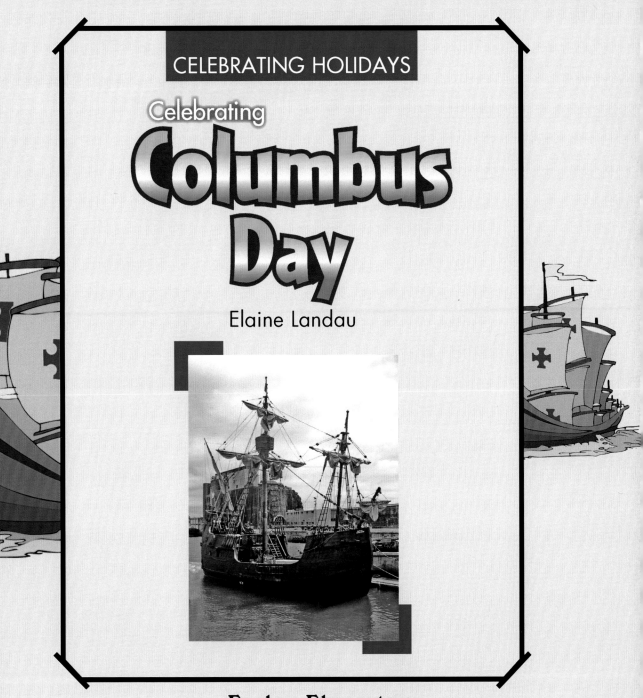

CELEBRATING HOLIDAYS

Celebrating
Columbus
Day

Elaine Landau

Enslow Elementary

an imprint of

Enslow Publishers, Inc.

40 Industrial Road
Box 398
Berkeley Heights, NJ 07922
USA

http://www.enslow.com

For Aaron Herschberg

Enslow Elementary, an imprint of Enslow Publishers, Inc.

Enslow Elementary® is a registered trademark of Enslow Publishers, Inc.

Original edition published as *Columbus Day: Celebrating a Famous Explorer* in 2001.

Library of Congress Cataloging-in-Publication Data

Landau, Elaine.
    Celebrating Columbus Day / Elaine Landau.
       p. cm.—(Celebrating holidays)
       Summary: "Read about Christopher Columbus, the discovery of America and how we celebrate this famous explorer"—Provided by publisher.
    Includes bibliographical references and index.
    ISBN 978-0-7660-4033-5 (alk. paper)
       1. Columbus Day—Juvenile literature. 2. Columbus, Christopher—Juvenile literature.
       3. America—Discovery and exploration—Spanish—Juvenile literature. I. Title.
  E120.L258 2012
  394.264—dc23   2011021327

Future Editions
Paperback ISBN 978-1-59845-400-0
ePUB ISBN 978-1-4645-1084-7
PDF ISBN 978-1-4646-1084-4

Printed in the United States of America

012012 The HF Group, North Manchester, IN

10 9 8 7 6 5 4 3 2 1

Photo Credits: © Artville, pp. 6, 10, 13; © Clipart.com, pp. 3, 14, 22; © Corel Corporation, Inc., p. 41; © Enslow Publishers, Inc., p. 26; Library of Congress, pp. 4, 7, 12, 16, 18, 19, 27, 32; National Aeronautics and Space Administration (NASA), p. 43; © 2010 Photos.com, a division of Getty Images. All rights reserved., pp. 9, 15, 23, 24, 27, 29, 32, 35, 38; © Shutterstock.com, pp. 5, 11, 20 (middle, bottom), 28, 30, 34, 36, 37, 39, 44; United States Department of Defense/Photographer MC2 Torrey W. Lee, p. 40; United States Mint, p. 42; Wikipedia, pp. 8, 17, 20.

Cover Photo: AP Images/Amy Sussman

CONTENTS

CHRISTOPHER·COLVMBVS

This is what one painter thought Christopher Columbus looked like as a young man. No one really knew what Columbus looked like.

CHAPTER 1

CHRISTOPHER COLUMBUS

Hundreds of years ago a man from Genoa, Italy, dreamed of sailing to an unknown place. That man was Christopher Columbus.

Columbus is famous for crossing the Atlantic Ocean by ship to reach the Americas. This was a whole new world that people in Europe did not know about. But Columbus had not really hoped to find that part of the world. When he left Europe, he was looking for a way to get to Asia by sea. There were many new and exciting things in Asia. Columbus hoped to bring back some of them when he returned home.

QUEST FOR ASIA

When Christopher Columbus left from Europe, he was looking for a way to get to Asia by sea. He hoped to bring back some of the new and exciting things from Asia.

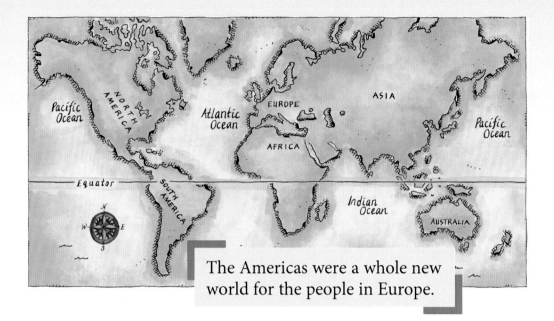

The Americas were a whole new world for the people in Europe.

Instead of reaching Asia, Columbus landed on an island in the Caribbean Sea that is now one of the islands of the West Indies. Columbus traveled to the New World four times between 1492 and 1504 to explore the West Indies. He also explored the coasts of Central America and South America.

Some people think that Columbus discovered America, but this is not quite true. The American Indians living there had arrived many years earlier. Columbus was not even the first European to sail there. In about A.D. 1000, Viking adventurers landed on the coast of North America. But they did not stay very long. The Vikings lived in the area that is now Denmark, Norway, and Sweden.

Columbus's trips led to a lasting link between Europe and the Americas. In time, other explorers followed, and trade and colonies grew. People's lives on both sides of the Atlantic Ocean were forever changed, and Christopher Columbus earned a place in history.

We remember Christopher Columbus each year on the second Monday in October. That is because Columbus landed in the West Indies on October 12, 1492.

American Indians had arrived many years earlier than Columbus. American Indians can be seen fishing as Columbus's ships arrive.

GENVA

Genoa as it looked when Columbus was a boy.

CHAPTER 2

IN THE BEGINNING

Christopher Columbus was born in 1451 in Genoa, Italy, a busy seaport on Italy's northwest coast.

We call him Christopher Columbus, but that is not what his parents called him. They named their child Christoforo Colombo. That is his name in Italian. Later, Columbus would go to Spain where he would be known as Cristobal Colón. That is his name in Spanish.

We do not know very much about Columbus's childhood, but we do know Columbus had four brothers and sisters. He was especially close to his brothers Bartholomew and Diego. They played together when they were children. As adults, they would often work together.

COLUMBUS AS A CHILD

No one really ever thought that Christopher Columbus would someday become a famous explorer. His father and grandfather were wool weavers. But his father wanted his eldest son to do more. He hoped that Christopher would someday become a very important businessman.

Trading was a successful business in Genoa. Many traders in Genoa made a great deal of money. They traveled to distant lands where they bought and sold many different things.

Columbus might have been a successful trader. As a boy he studied math and a language called Latin. Later, he wanted to do many things. But it took a lot of money to become a trader. So, at first, Columbus worked for a man who was a trader.

By the 1470s, Columbus had gone on several trading trips. He went to France in Europe, Tunisia in Africa, and other countries. He learned about trading and he also learned about sailing. He liked sailing the best.

By the 1470s, Columbus had gone on several trading trips. He went to France in Europe, Tunisia in Africa and other countries.

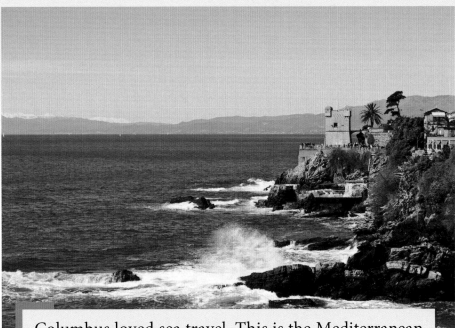

Columbus loved sea travel. This is the Mediterranean Sea near Genoa where Columus was born.

Columbus moved from Italy to Portugal in 1476. We are not sure why he moved. According to the story, he was trying to get to England when pirates attacked his ship near Portugal. Columbus may have been hurt.

Christopher Columbus was not alone once he got to Portugal. His brother Bartholomew was there. Like Christopher, Bartholomew Columbus loved sea travel. Bartholomew and Christopher Columbus designed and sold maps to traders.

The Columbus brothers lived in Lisbon, Portugal, a very busy seaport. Ships were always coming into Lisbon.

People used spices like pepper, cloves, cinnamon, and nutmeg to season food. These spices could be found in the Indies.

There were many chances to sail to distant places. Christopher Columbus sometimes sailed to those places.

He did other things, too. He married a young woman named Felipa Perestrello de Moniz in 1479. A year later they had a son they named Diego. Felipa's father was governor of Porto Santo, a Portuguese island off the coast of northern Africa. Columbus lived there with his wife and child for a while.

In the early 1480s, Columbus sailed to the Canary Islands. This is a group of islands off the Western coast of Africa. He also visited West Africa. There he learned about the trade in slaves, gold, and gems like diamonds.

Columbus knew that what European traders needed most was a safe and shorter route to Asia. That was where India, Japan, China, and the East Indies were. These countries had gold, silk, and spices. Spices, like cloves and nutmeg, were not only put in food. They were also used as medicines, and people paid a lot of money for them.

But Asia was extremely hard to get to. It was a long and costly trip by land. Travelers were often attacked by bandits along the way.

It was not an easy sea voyage either. Sailors reached Asia in a roundabout way. They sailed south and then east around Africa. The passage was difficult and dangerous. Many ships were wrecked in storms at sea. Pirates sometimes attacked these vessels. The pirates knew that the ships carried valuable things.

Columbus studied all his maps and charts. Finally he came up with a new route to Asia. He wanted to sail west rather than east. Columbus thought this would shorten the trip. After all, the earth is round. So sailors should be able to get to Asia from either direction.

At first no one believed Columbus. Some people think Columbus was not believed because he said

During Columbus's time, people called the countries of India, China, and Japan the Indies. This is what the map looks like today.

the earth was round. That is not true. Smart people already knew that the earth was round. People did not believe Columbus for another reason.

Columbus thought the world was smaller than it was. That made him sure that Asia was much closer to Europe than it really was. There were other problems with Columbus's plan, too. The earth is covered with mostly water. But Columbus's maps showed it was covered with mostly land. He believed that Asia stretched farther east than it does.

The earth is covered mostly with water. But Columbus's maps showed it was covered with mostly land.

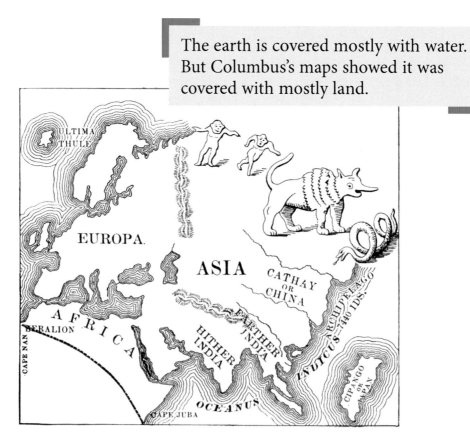

Columbus also thought sailing west was the best way to go. That was wrong, too. Two large bodies of land blocked his path. Those areas of land were North and South America. Columbus did not know anything about these continents. Many years before, Viking explorer Leif Eriksson had landed in North America, but he had not realized where he was. And his people never settled the land. To Columbus, it was still new territory that had never been explored.

Christopher Columbus wished to try out his new route. But he needed people to help pay for the costly voyage. He had to have at least three ships to carry enough food, water, and supplies for a long trip. First he had to make others believe that he was right.

Today we know that Columbus never reached Asia. Instead, he found something far more valuable.

Columbus wished to try out his new route. He had to have at least three ships to carry enough food, water, and supplies for the long trip.

Columbus spent many years
getting ready for his trip.

CHAPTER 3

MAKING THE DREAM COME TRUE

Christopher Columbus was determined to prove his ideas. In 1483 he met with King John II of Portugal. Columbus hoped the king would help pay for his voyage. But the king turned Columbus down. The king was sure Columbus would never reach Asia. Columbus still believed he could. He refused to give up.

The years ahead were difficult for Columbus. Many people laughed at his ideas. His wife died sometime between 1484 and 1485. Discouraged, Columbus left Portugal with his son, Diego, and went to Spain.

COLUMBUS SETS SAIL

A total of ninety men were onboard Columbus's three ships, including two of his brothers, Bartholomew and Diego. Most of the men were sailors. However, each ship also had a doctor. There was also a bookkeeper to keep track of the supplies, as well as a translator. Columbus had to be able to talk to the people in Asia, and he did not know how to speak their languages.

The years ahead were difficult for Columbus.
Many people laughed at his ideas.

In 1486, Columbus went before King Ferdinand and
Queen Isabella of Spain. He asked them if they would
help pay for his voyage to Asia. The queen liked
Columbus. She also liked the idea of finding a faster
way to get to Asia. Yet, her advisers told her it was
impossible. They realized that the world was larger
than Columbus thought it was. They also knew that
the earth had more water than land. Once again, the
royal advisers were right. And, as before, Columbus
did not believe them.

This time he was luckier. Queen Isabella was not quite convinced that Columbus was wrong. One other person advising the queen thought Columbus might be right. That person was the royal treasurer, Luís de Santangel. At the time, Spain did not have enough money to help pay for Columbus's voyage. However, the queen did not definitely say Spain would refuse to help.

Queen Isabella of Spain, along with King Ferdinand, listen as Columbus (standing) speaks.

Columbus had three ships for his voyage, *Niña* (top), the *Pinta* (middle), and the *Santa María* (bottom). These ships are modern-day replicas.

Niña

Santa María

Pinta

Columbus waited and hoped. He continued to talk to the queen about the trip. He also looked for other people who could help pay for the trip. He went back to Portugal to ask King John II again for help, but the king still refused. Columbus asked his brother Bartholomew to help. Bartholomew traveled to different countries looking for people who would be willing to help pay for the trip. He was turned down in both England and France.

Then in the spring of 1492 things changed. Spain had won a war. Now it had money for Columbus's voyage. Some people think that Queen Isabella sold her jewels to help, but that never happened. Luís de Santangel urged the queen to help pay for Columbus's voyage, and she took his advice.

Columbus excitedly prepared for the voyage. He had three ships—the *Niña*, the *Pinta* and the *Santa María*. Columbus was captain of the *Santa María*, the largest ship. But his favorite ship was the *Niña*. It was lighter and faster than the other two ships.

The wooden ships were not like the modern ships of today. Back then, ships did not have engines. So the crew had to move the ships using ropes and sails. Only the officers had sleeping quarters. The sailors found places to sleep on the open deck. In bad weather they slept down below. The food was not the best either. The men ate salty meat or fish and hard biscuits. They drank wine mixed with water. On August 3, 1492, Columbus's three ships left Palos, Spain. The first stop was the Canary Islands. There the ships would be stocked with fresh food, water, and wood. The wood was used to do some repair work on the *Pinta*. The *Niña*'s sails were replaced with stronger ones.

On September 6 the voyage continued. At first the crew felt lucky. The winds were strong and in their favor. The ships made good time. But after about a month things changed. The men wondered why they had not reached land yet.

Crew members on Columbus's ships had heard stories about horrible sea monsters.

Fear spread among the men on the three ships. All had heard stories about horrible sea monsters. Now they wondered if these stories could be true. Many felt they would never reach Asia. And they were afraid of running out of food and water.

The men did not fight Columbus. But Columbus knew they were close to it. If that happened, he might be thrown overboard. So Columbus made a bargain with his crew. He asked them to give him a few more days. If they did not reach land, he would turn the ships around. We will never know if Columbus would have kept his word.

Columbus made a bargain with his crew. He asked them to give him a few more days to see if land appeared.

When they reached land, Columbus and his men went off to explore.

Hopeful signs began to appear soon after Columbus spoke with his crew. Land birds were seen flying overhead. A tree branch was spotted in the water. Someone saw a large piece of wood in the sea. It looked as though it had been carved. Land was near, and it was finally spotted on October 12, 1492. The men celebrated by firing cannons into the air. Columbus thought his dream had come true. He dressed in his finest clothes to leave the ship and explore the land. He was sure he was in the East Indies. He could not have been more wrong. Once again, he did not know it.

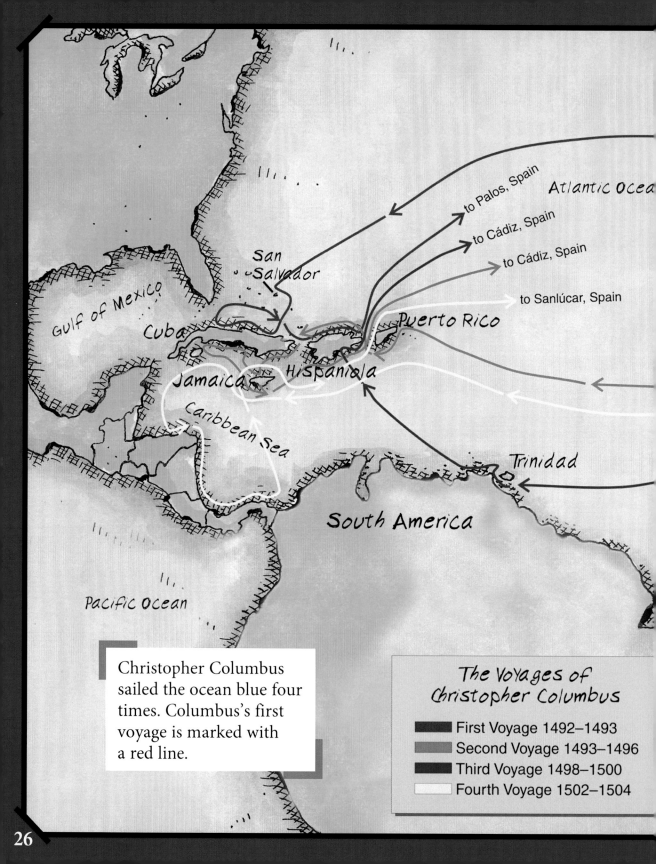

to Palos, Spain

Atlantic Ocean

to Cádiz, Spain

to Cádiz, Spain

to Sanlúcar, Spain

San Salvador

Gulf of Mexico

Cuba

Puerto Rico

Jamaica

Hispaniola

Caribbean Sea

Trinidad

South America

Pacific Ocean

Christopher Columbus sailed the ocean blue four times. Columbus's first voyage is marked with a red line.

The Voyages of Christopher Columbus

First Voyage 1492–1493
Second Voyage 1493–1496
Third Voyage 1498–1500
Fourth Voyage 1502–1504

CHAPTER 4

THE
NEW WORLD

Christopher Columbus was nowhere near Asia. He was in the West Indies. These islands are just southeast of Florida on the east coast of the United States. The native people there were farmers. They grew their own food and wove cloth. They lived in peaceful villages. Columbus called the native people Indians because he thought he was in the East Indies.

The Indians helped the visitors. They gave Columbus and his men food. They offered the men shelter and showed them the island. But their kindness was not returned.

MEETING NEW PEOPLE

The Tainos were friendly but they only had food and water to offer Columbus and his crew rather than (in contrast to what is shown in the illustration) gold.

An Indian sees Columbus's ships coming near land. Columbus called the people Indians because he thought he was in the East Indies.

In time, Columbus and his men mistreated the Indians. They made them work long hours and gave them little food. If the Indians disobeyed, they were harshly punished. Many died from the lack of food and the cruel treatment they received. Some Indians died of diseases the Europeans brought with them. Columbus had also brought Christianity to the Indians. He thought that this made up for what the Indians lost, but he was wrong.

At first, the Indians helped the visitors. However, Columbus and his men were not so kind.

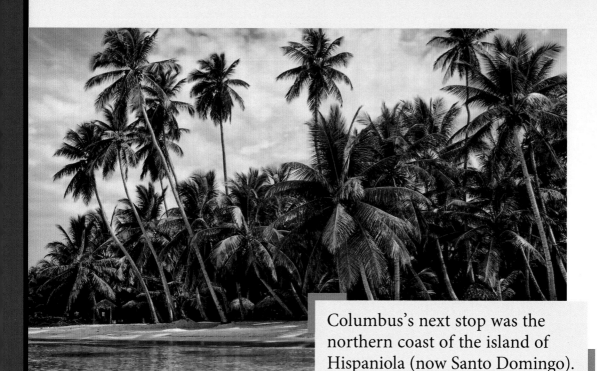

Columbus's next stop was the northern coast of the island of Hispaniola (now Santo Domingo).

Columbus wanted to explore the entire area. He still believed he was in Asia. He forced some of the Indians onto his ship to serve as guides. He also hoped to bring them back to Spain to impress the king and queen.

Columbus left some of his men on the island and set sail with the others. His next stop was the northern coast of the island of Hispaniola. Columbus took control of it and claimed it for Spain. He also traveled to Cuba. He thought it might be Japan. In Cuba he found a small amount of gold.

Columbus continued his travels. He hoped to find China before returning to Spain, but his plans were cut short. On Christmas Eve Columbus went to bed early. A sailor was told to remain at the ship's wheel, to keep it on course. He did not; he ordered a cabin boy to do so instead. The young boy crashed the ship into dry land. The *Santa María* was wrecked on a reef near Haiti.

Once again the native people on the island helped Columbus. The explorer left about forty of his men in Haiti to build a fort and search for gold. The *Santa María* could not be repaired, so Columbus abandoned the ship.

The *Niña* and *Pinta* headed for Spain. The trip was extremely difficult. Some of the Indians on the ships died. And there were terrible storms at sea.

When he got to Spain, Columbus was treated like a king. There were feasts in his honor. King Ferdinand and Queen Isabella gave Columbus an official title. He was now "Admiral of the Ocean Seas and Viceroy of the Indies."

The king and queen also ordered a second voyage to the New World. That would not be Columbus's last trip. In all, Columbus made four trips there.

Columbus was treated like a king when he returned to Spain from his voyage.

He explored the islands of Puerto Rico, Trinidad, and Jamaica. He explored parts of Central America and South America as well.

Columbus never found the riches he dreamed of. He also had many disappointments and suffered many hardships before dying in 1506. By then, he knew there was no quick route to Asia. But he never realized one important thing: He had opened the door to a whole new world.

Closeup of Columbus Statue, Barcelona, Spain

CHAPTER 5

REMEMBERING COLUMBUS

Christopher Columbus sailed to the New World. But we do not live in Columbia. We live in America. The continents of North and South America were not named for Columbus. They were named for another Italian explorer named Amerigo Vespucci.

Christopher Columbus was not forgotten. A South American country was named for him. It is the Republic of Colombia. The capital of the United States is Washington, D.C. The D.C. stands for District of Columbia. There is Columbus, Ohio, and Columbus, Georgia. Many other cities, streets, schools, and buildings in the United States have Columbus's name.

CELEBRATING

One of the largest Columbus Day celebrations was called the World's Columbian Exposition. This was a fabulous world's fair in Chicago, Illinois. There were many interesting displays. These included actual-size models of Columbus's three ships. However, the fair required quite a bit of work. As a result, a whole year of preparations took place before the fair could open.

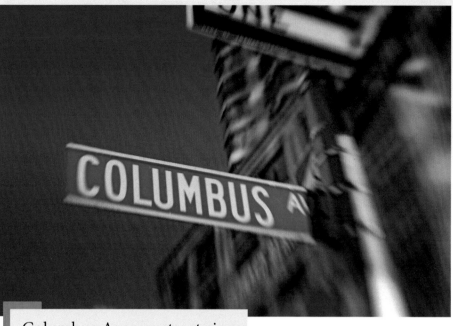

Columbus Avenue street sign in New York City.

There are also statues and monuments to honor Christopher Columbus. Paintings of him hang in many buildings. Often museums and libraries have exhibits about Columbus. Some trace his route to the Americas.

Yet, we did not always celebrate Columbus Day. The first official Columbus Day celebration was held on October 12, 1792. That was the three hundredth anniversary of Columbus's landing. A group known as the Society of St. Tammany, or the Colombian Order, planned it.

The idea did not catch on right away. There were only small celebrations in different parts of the country. Often Italian-American groups sponsored these gatherings. The Italian Americans were proud that Columbus was Italian.

The next large Columbus Day celebration was in 1892. It was the four hundredth anniversary of Columbus's arrival. President Benjamin Harrison of the United States liked the idea. He asked Americans everywhere to celebrate. Schools put on shows about Columbus. Community centers had parties and dances. A ballet called *Columbus and the Discovery of America* was even written.

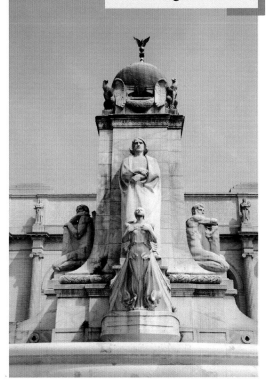

Columbus Statue, Union Station, Washington, D.C.

After 1892, Columbus Day was celebrated more regularly. Some people felt it should be an official holiday. They asked their state lawmakers to declare Columbus Day an official holiday.

This is a painting of Columbus.

In 1909, New York became the first state to do so. On October 12 the governor led a grand parade. There have been Columbus Day parades in New York ever since.

There have been Columbus Day parades in other places as well. Many states also made Columbus Day a legal holiday. Usually a parade was part of the celebration. Finally, in 1971, Columbus Day became a federal holiday. This means that on October 12 all government offices are closed. There is no mail delivery. Many businesses and schools do not open. It is supposed to be a day of celebration in honor of Christopher Columbus.

Not everyone celebrates. American Indians do not feel that Columbus was a hero. They dislike the cruel treatment their people received from Columbus

In some cities in the United States an Etnic Diversity Day has taken the place of Columbus Day activities in some areas.

and his men. In some cities American Indians have protested Columbus Day. They want to replace it with a different holiday that honors all Americans.

This new holiday is already celebrated in many Latin American countries. On October 12 those countries celebrate Día de la Raza (Day of the Race). This is a celebration of all people and of Columbus's voyages. There are usually parades, festivals, and speeches. In some cities in the United States things are changing, too. "Ethnic Diversity Day" has taken the place of Columbus Day activities in some areas.

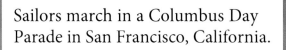

Sailors march in a Columbus Day Parade in San Francisco, California.

CHAPTER 6

CELEBRATING YOUR WAY

How is Columbus Day celebrated? Most towns and cities have parades. Some places do more. Farmingdale, Long Island, in New York, has an annual Columbus Weekend Fair. This includes a carnival, barbecue, and live music. Stores have sidewalk sales. There is a magic show for children, and the event ends with fireworks.

Columbus Day is fun on Jack Frost Mountain in Pennsylvania. There is an arts and crafts festival. Over seventy artists take part. You can ride a chairlift up the mountain. And there is always lots of good food.

IN THE SKY

In the city of Columbus, Kansas Columbus Day is celebrated with a three-day festival. People go for hot-air balloon rides.

The city of Columbus, Kansas, celebrates in a big way. It hosts a fun-filled three-day festival. There is a Miss Columbus pageant and a classic car show. People go for hot-air balloon rides.

Some groups in Berkeley, California, celebrate in a different way. They enjoy Indigenous People's Day. This is a celebration of American-Indian cultures. There are Indian-American dances, foods, and crafts.

The city of Columbus, Ohio, has been true to its name. It built a model of the *Santa María*. Actors there play the parts of the people from the voyage.

Christopher Columbus Quincentenary Silver Dollar

Visitors can meet the actors and see the inner workings of the ship. They can hear how cannon fire signaled the *Niña* or *Pinta*. It is the next best thing to sailing with Columbus.

Columbus Day is a good time to think about the past. But it is a good time to think about the future as well. Much has changed through the years. Today there are new frontiers to explore.

In the fifteenth century, people explored the sea and the land. Now we are exploring space. Would Columbus have wanted to visit Mars? Would he have come up with a shorter route to get there? Whole new universes await us. Perhaps you will be among those who help explore them.

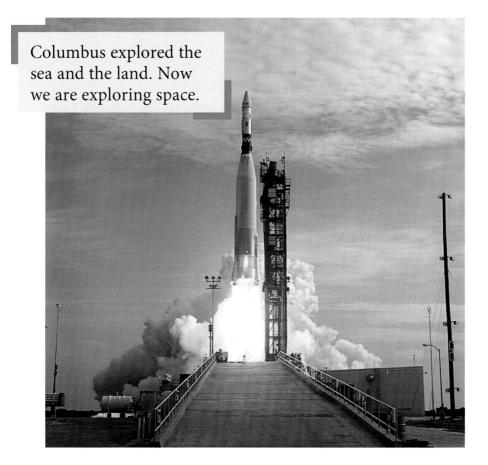

Columbus explored the sea and the land. Now we are exploring space.

Columbus Day Craft Project

Sailboat

Christopher Columbus liked to sail. This project will show you how to make your own small boat. You will need:

- ✳ **a three-inch square of paper**
- ✳ **crayons or markers**
- ✳ **a toothpick**
- ✳ **a small piece of clay**
- ✳ **a walnut shell**

1 Decorate the paper square with the crayons or markers. Make it as colorful as you like. It will be the boat's sail.

2 With the toothpick, poke two holes in the paper. Push the toothpick through one hole and out the other.

3 Roll the clay into a ball. Place it firmly in the middle of the inside of the walnut shell.

4 Stick the end of the toothpick in the clay. The sail should stand up straight. Now your boat is ready to float in the sink or in a bowl of water.

*Safety Note: Be sure to ask for help from an adult, if needed, to complete this project.

Words to Know

anniversary—The day each year when a past event is celebrated.

cargo—The goods carried by a ship, airplane, truck, or other vehicle.

continent—One of the seven large land areas on the earth.

explorer—A person who travels to unknown places.

native—A person who was born in the country in which he or she lives.

New World—The name sometimes used for North and South America.

territory—Any large area of land.

vessel—A ship, or large boat.

voyage—A trip by water or through space.

Read More About

Aloian, Molly. *Columbus Day*. New York, New York: Crabtree Publishing Company, 2010.

Ansary, Mir Tamim. *Columbus Day*. Mankota, Minnesota: Heinemann-Raintree, 2007.

Nelson, Robin. *Columbus Day*. Minneapolis, Minnesota: Lerner Publishing Group, 2009.

Internet Addresses

Enchanted Learning
<http://www.enchantedlearning.com/crafts/columbus/>
Learn about geography and history while doing fun projects.

Kaboose
<http://holidays.kaboose.com/columbus-day/>
Join in the celebration with a selection of crafts, history lessons, recipes, games and Columbus Day printables.

TimeandDate
<http://www.timeanddate.com/holidays/us/columbus-day>
Explore the history of Columbus Day, which is annually the second Monday of October in the United States.

Index